NATIVE AMERICAN

RED JACKET

BY MARIA NELSON

 Gareth Stevens
PUBLISHING

Please visit our website, www.garethstevens.com. For a free color catalog of all our high-quality books, call toll free 1-800-542-2595 or fax 1-877-542-2596.

Library of Congress Cataloging-in-Publication Data

Nelson, Maria.
 Red Jacket / Maria Nelson.
     pages cm. — (Native American heroes)
 Includes bibliographical references and index.
 ISBN 978-1-4824-2696-0 (pbk.)
 ISBN 978-1-4824-2697-7 (6 pack)
 ISBN 978-1-4824-2698-4 (library binding)
 1. Red Jacket (Seneca chief), approximately 1756-1830—Juvenile literature. 2.
 Seneca Indians—Kings and rulers—Biography—Juvenile literature. I. Title.
 E99.S3N44 2015
 974.7004'975546—dc23
 [B]

                              2015006058

Published in 2016 by
Gareth Stevens Publishing
111 East 14th Street, Suite 349
New York, NY 10003

Copyright © 2016 Gareth Stevens Publishing

Designer: Laura Bowen
Editor: Kristen Rajczak

Photo credits: Cover, p. 1 Universal History Archive/Universal Images Group/
Getty Images; cover, pp. 1–24 (series art) Binkski/Shutterstock.com; pp. 5, 7
Stock Montage/Archive Photos/Getty Images; p. 9 blinkblink/Shutterstock.com;
p. 11 Kean Collection/Archive Photos/Getty Images; p. 13 Eliot Elisofon/
The LIFE Picture Collection/Getty Images; p. 15 SuperStock/Getty Images;
p. 17 Thomas Hicks/Wikimedia Commons; p. 19 Print Collector/Hulton Archive/
Getty Images; p. 21 Dave Pape/Wikimedia Commons.

Printed in the United States of America

CPSIA compliance information: Batch #CS15GS: For further information contact Gareth Stevens, New York, New York at 1-800-542-2595.

CONTENTS

Boldface words appear in the glossary.

Brave Speaker

After the founding of the United States, Native Americans lost land to the new country. Some, such as Chief Red Jacket, tried to work with the US government to stop this. He showed bravery by speaking up for his people!

5

Early Life

Red Jacket was born around 1758 in central New York. The exact place and date aren't certain. At birth, his name was Otetiani. When he became a chief during the 1790s, he took the name Sagoyewatha (SAY-goh-yeh-WAY-thuh).

7

Red Jacket was part of the Seneca nation. The Seneca were part of a larger group called the **Iroquois Confederacy**. By the time Red Jacket was born, the confederacy had six nations in it. The Seneca nation was the largest.

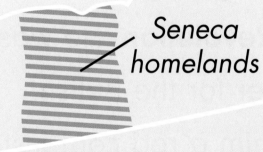

CANADA

VT

NY

MA

Lake Ontario

Seneca homelands

CT

Lake Erie

PA

NJ

UNITED STATES

The Red Coat

Red Jacket earned his English name while fighting in the **American Revolution**. He was a **messenger** for the British. They gave him a red coat just like the British soldiers wore.

Red Jacket ran away from a few battles during the war. Some people called him a **coward**! But Red Jacket was a great **orator**. He made up for his actions by speaking for his people's rights after the war.

13

Rising to Power

Red Jacket's speaking skills and **negotiations** with the US government helped him become chief! In 1792, Red Jacket met with George Washington to talk about Seneca problems, such as their loss of land. Washington gave him a silver peace medal.

On the Other Side

The United States fought the British again in the War of 1812. This time, Red Jacket was on the American side. He fought bravely, even though he was getting older. No one called him a coward then!

17

Many Seneca and other Iroquois died in the War of 1812. Native American leaders chose to withdraw from the war and stop the deaths of their people. Red Jacket played a big part in this decision.

Remembered Today

Red Jacket remained a Seneca chief into the 1820s! He continued to speak up for the needs of his people. Red Jacket died in 1830 on the Buffalo Creek **Reservation** in western New York.

THE LIFE OF RED JACKET

1758 — Red Jacket is born.

1775–1782 — Senecas fight on the side of the British in the American Revolution. Red Jacket is a messenger for the British.

1792 — George Washington gives Red Jacket a peace medal.

1812 — The War of 1812 begins.

1830 — Red Jacket dies January 20.

GLOSSARY

American Revolution: the war in which the colonies won their freedom from England

coward: someone who is easily scared

Iroquois Confederacy: a group of Native American tribes living in present-day New York who worked and acted together

messenger: someone who carries notes between two groups or people

negotiation: the act of coming to an agreement

orator: one who gives speeches, especially in a formal setting

reservation: land set aside by the US government for Native Americans

FOR MORE INFORMATION

BOOKS

Hinton, Kaavonia. *The Iroquois of the Northeast.* Kennett Square, PA: Purple Toad Publishing, Inc., 2013.

Sonneborn, Liz. *The American Indian Experience.* Minneapolis, MN: Twenty-First Century Books, 2011.

WEBSITES

Historic Seneca Leaders
sni.org/culture/historic-seneca-leaders/
Read about Red Jacket and other great leaders of the Seneca tribe.

Seneca Indian Fact Sheet
www.bigorrin.org/seneca_kids.htm
Learn more about the Senecas.

INDEX